Master Studies
by Joe Morello

edited by Rick Mattingly

Modern Drummer Publisher / CEO - **David Frangioni**

President - **David Hakim**

Senior Art Director - **Scott Bienstock**

Original Design and Layout David Creamer
Updated Layout and Notation Terry Branam
Cover Photography Rick Mattingly

Special thanks to:
Dom Famularo, John Riley, Danny Gottlieb,
Steve Forster, Debbie Andreas, Jerry Bogner,
Joe Bergamini, Claus Hessler, Frank Perry,
Nic Kubes, Val Suprenamt, Martin Roser, Michael Scott

© Copyright 1983, 2000, 2022 Modern Drummer Media, LLC.
International Copyright Secured
All Rights Reserved
Printed in the USA

Any unauthorized duplication of this book or
its contents is a violation of copyright laws.

Published by:
Modern Drummer Media, LLC.
1279 W Palmetto Park Rd
PO Box 276064
Boca Raton, FL 33427

Subscribe to *Modern Drummer*: moderndummer.com/subscribe

For videos, visit and subscribe to the "Modern Drummer Official" YouTube channel

Dedication

Although the actual writing of this book began about ten years ago, in concept it was born many years earlier, while I was studying with Mr. George Lawrence Stone of Boston. At that time, the only book Mr. Stone had to his credit was *Stick Control*, which I practiced religiously. However, being a bit precocious, I would frequently experiment with different ways to practice my assignments. At my lesson each week, I would show these ideas to Mr. Stone and ask his opinion of them. He always seemed to enjoy them, and one day, he honored me with the dedication of his second book, *Accents And Rebounds*, which he claimed was inspired by some of my experiments.

Still not satisfied, Mr. Stone suggested that I rewrite *Stick Control*. I told Mr. Stone that I felt *Stick Control* was perfect just the way it was. I would never consider rewriting it, but I would love to collaborate on a new book with him. Unfortunately, my hectic tour schedule and Mr. Stone's untimely passing turned this dream into an impossibility.

I therefore dedicate this book to Mr. George Lawrence Stone, and to my other two teachers, Joseph D. Sefcik and Billy Gladstone, and to my wife, Jean Ann.

Joe Morello

A NOTE FROM THE PUBLISHER

I started playing drums at age 2, getting serious about practicing by age 8. My earliest drum heroes were Buddy Rich, Carl Palmer and our subject here within, Joe Morello. From my earliest years of listening to Joe play on Dave Brubeck records, I was in near disbelief of Joe's playing, his precision, musicality and incredible finesse. As I dove deeper into his story, I quickly learned that Joe himself, never stopped learning! He was a true, lifelong student of drumming.

The moment I was old enough to study with Joe, I impatiently waited for his classified ad in *Modern Drummer* to appear offering an opening for students. The challenge was that he taught in New Jersey, and I lived in Boston. What was a 15-year-old with little funds to do? Take the cheapest airplane flight possible and ask Joe to provide 3-hour lessons each trip! My journey studying with Joe began there, resumed for years in person (eventually I could drive there!) and to this day, through Master Studies I & II, continues in spirit and in practice. Dom Famularo, *Modern Drummer* head of worldwide education and my teacher, studied intensely with Joe and continues the in-person teaching that Joe pioneered.

Here we are decades after Joe hit the charts with "Take Five" and many years into *Master Studies*, the material has proven to be as timeless and incredible as Joe's legacy. A true honor to present my teacher and soon to be yours, Joe Morello *Master Studies*.

David Frangioni
CEO/Publisher of Modern Drummer Publications, Inc.

Contents

Introduction

by Jim Chapin

Quite a complicated recipe, this making of a drummer: the ability to maintain an even tempo; a firm sense of meter; good coordination between hands and feet; quick reflexes; the self-discipline that enables one to practice hard and with concentration.

These are fundamental building blocks, and any young drummer should consider himself blessed if he starts his career with a sizable chunk of even one of them. Even the greatest players make it clear that, in spite of their success, the preponderance of their talent usually lies in but one or two of the above areas.

This is what makes Joe Morello so amazing. He has no visible weaknesses. His time is impeccable; his taste is unerringly correct with reflexes like lightning. And his coordination, on many different levels, is unique.

On top of what must have been an outstanding original talent, the fact that Joe is one of the world's champion practicers is also largely responsible. Many drummers have conditioned themselves, sometimes grudgingly, to be with their drums for some appreciable portion of their waking hours. Joe, who has been playing drums for over thirty years, is still in the first flush of a great love affair with the instrument.

Joe first studied with Joe Sefcik in his hometown of Springfield, Massachusetts. Sefcik was a remarkable teacher who gave him a fine background, and then suggested Joe study with George Lawrence Stone, a delightful man, who was just overjoyed with Joe. Of course, the lessons proved to be just as rewarding for the teacher as the pupil.

When I spent a day with Mr. Stone in 1951, he talked about "the outstanding kid from Springfield" a good part of the time. Of course, I didn't connect the "drum monster" I met at the Valley Arena that very next year with Stone's prize pupil.

As far back as the mid-'50s, Joe was far along in the process of developing his own special and devastating technique, a skill which has given rise to some marvelous drum mythology: "Man, I never heard anything like it! That cat was rolling with his left hand!" This technique might be characterized as a sort of perpetual motion of evenly divided three- or four-note phrases.

Many drummers make a rough attempt at this effect by first dragging the stick, in a kind of repeated buzz, and then opening it, trying vainly to produce evenly divided accented taps. Superficially, it might be said that Joe does the same thing, but in contrast, his sound is perfectly "round," with no breaks in continuity.

Probably, it is Joe's most amazing invention, but perhaps some credit belongs to the late Billy Gladstone and his theory of "catching the bounce." Joe took only a few lessons from Gladstone, but all he has ever needed was the spark of an idea from which to build an imposing edifice.

Speed? Joe can perform with one hand what others need two hands or more to achieve. How did he arrive at this pinnacle? Talent, energy—and an analytical mind.

New York's Hickory House was a jazz and steak house for about forty years. From late 1952 until 1955, when he left Marian McPartland to join Dave Brubeck, Joe held open drum clinics there. Sitting at the oval bar that enclosed the bandstand entitled a young drummer to more than the trio; during the intermissions, one could follow Joe to a rear table to watch him perform miracles on a folded napkin.

In his first few months in New York, Joe's intense interest in drums and his natural modesty often conspired to get him in trouble. In perfect innocence and admiration, Joe would ask some respectable, though perhaps not overwhelming, technician to demonstrate a facet of his learning. Falling into the trap, and without any idea of Joe's capabilities, the "master" would display his technique. In all sincerity, Joe would enthusiastically ask, "Is this right?" and then proceed to reproduce whatever had been demonstrated—twice as fast and much cleaner!

Until the pecking order had been established, and Joe's original position as "new boy in town" had turned into unchallenged "king of the hill," his sincere thirst for knowledge made some unwary drummers quite nervous.

The Dave Brubeck Quartet had acquired a respectable following of jazz fans well before Joe joined the group. Their concerts were sellouts all over the country. However, Joe brought a new solo voice into the fray, along with the facility and flexibility to anticipate and complement Brubeck's search for new rhythmic directions in jazz. Many composers in the pop field learned their lessons well at the feet of these master experimenters.

During the Brubeck years, Joe produced a body of recorded solos that has no parallel in all jazz. In addition to all the technical excellence on display, the final impression is one of delightful discovery. The solos are so full of episode, of delicious surprises, and of theme and variation that they stand on their own as drum compositions.

Joe has maintained a lower profile recently, concentrating on teaching and cutting down on personal appearances. But hearing Joe today is a real revelation. He is a veritable powerhouse. Part of this relatively recent step forward is his increased use and understanding of the Moeller system, which he was forced to achieve from a distance and almost by intuition.

Sanford Moeller, through years of observation, had discovered that there was a common trait that "swift" drummers seemed to share: the look of the hands and arms in relationship to the sticks. The action of the "thrown" accents made it appear as though the sticks had a secret power of their own. The exercises that Moeller invented and compiled utilized the extraordinary acceleration of whipping accents, and an axiom of physics: "An object in motion (in this case the tip of the stick), when allowed to move freely, tends to stay in motion." Moeller claimed no origination of the system, and he believed that really gifted students would eventually develop it naturally through trial and error.

Joe never studied with Moeller. In later years, Moeller developed a habit of discouraging students from enrolling for lessons. His rejection of Joe seems tragic in retrospect. Moeller would have been very proud to see what Joe has accomplished with his system, even from a distance. He has achieved standards of speed and dexterity that the "old man" could never have possibly anticipated.

The student of this present work will find a real, but realistic, challenge here. For shining out from each exercise is the light from the lively intelligence of Joe Morello—an all-time drumming genius.

Preface

by Joe Morello

on technique

Master Studies is not intended to be a "how-to" book. By that I mean that it's not an instruction book that will teach you various hand and stick positions, nor does this book have anything to do with any "style" of playing, nor is it intended to give the drummer some "hot licks." This is a workbook of material to use in developing the hands for accenting, and for controlling the different pressures used in single strokes, double strokes, and closed rolls. You can go through this book using whatever techniques you've been taught, and you can apply the ideas in this book to any style of music you want. Furthermore, this book does not have to be practiced in any particular order. You can skip around and work on whichever exercises are most appropriate to your needs at any given time.

Technique is only a means to an end. The goal is to play musically, but some drummers lose sight of this and approach the drums strictly from a technical standpoint. Often, they become so fascinated with speed that they miss the whole point of music. So just studying this book for the technique alone doesn't make any sense. You have to apply the technique to the music you are playing. If you need to use accents, for example, this book will help you develop the ability to put an accent wherever you hear one. But when you are playing, you should not be thinking, "Well, now I'm going to play page such-and-such from *Master Studies*." The ultimate goal is to be able to play what you hear in your mind and to be able to play it instantly.

Although I am known as a jazz drummer, I never studied jazz drumming with anyone. My teachers were Joseph D. Sefcik, George Lawrence Stone, and Billy Gladstone, who were not jazz drummers by any means, but who knew how to get a good sound out of a drum. In my travels around the world, I've run into many different approaches and techniques. I think it would be presumptuous of me to declare my way of playing as being the "end-all" of techniques. However, there is one thing that I want to make very clear: I've come to the conclusion that everything is done with natural body movement. The wrist turns and everything have to be natural; they have to fit the way the body is made. You must use everything in a natural way. After you have been playing awhile, you will develop an individualized style, and each style has its place.

Some of the things in this book are unusual, and they might give you different ideas about things you can do. For example, some of the accents are in odd places, and in that respect, it might open your mind to different patterns. But ultimately, it's up to your imagination to develop your own creativity. So this book is just to help you develop your facility, keep yourself in shape, and help you become aware of what your hands are doing and how they're working. How you use the technique is up to you.

using the metronome

I feel that the exercises in this book should be practiced with a metronome. But it is important to understand what a metronome will do and what it will not do.

A metronome will help you to be rhythmically accurate; it will not teach you to swing. The metronome can be used to gauge your development; it should not be used as a challenge. Let's look at each of these points.

The metronome is useful in teaching you to space your notes correctly and keep time. The metronome will not slow down when you play the fast parts; it won't speed up on the slow parts; it won't change the pulse when you change from 8ths to triplets to 16ths. It can be very valuable in helping you to learn rhythmic relationships (such as those in the "Table of Time" section in this book). It will also help prepare you for playing with a click track, if you should encounter one in a recording studio.

The metronome will not teach you to swing or groove. That has to do with feeling, and the metronome has no feeling; it's a machine. However, don't be afraid of the metronome either. There has been a myth going around for years that, if you practice with a metronome, you'll play mechanically. That's not true. So use the metronome as a guide, but don't let it become more important than it really is.

One way of using it as a guide is by gauging your progress with it. As your proficiency increases, you can play with the metronome set at higher tempos. Psychologically, being able to see your progress is helpful. But don't get involved in a speed contest with the metronome. When you forget about being musical and start worrying about speed, you are defeating the purpose of music. Being able to play 16th notes at a metronome setting of 270 doesn't mean a thing if you can't play them musically.

I suggest starting off slowly each time you practice. Make sure you are totally relaxed. After your muscles are warmed up, you can gradually increase the tempo, one metronome marking at a time. If, at any point, you start to feel tension in your hands, wrists, or arms, STOP. Move the metronome back a couple of notches and work from a tempo at which you are totally relaxed. This is what will eventually build speed.

We all have days when we don't seem to be able to play as well. Maybe yesterday you were able to play a certain exercise with the metronome set at 160, but today you feel tension if you try to go past 148. Fine. Stay at 148. Playing stiffly at 160 won't do you a bit of good. Eventually, you'll work your way back up to 160. Your top speed may go up and down from day to day, but if you average your speed and compare it week to week, you should see some improvement.

Experiment with using the metronome on different beats. You may want to start with the metronome clicking off each beat of the bar. But after you can do that, try it with the metronome clicking off only the first beat of each bar, or set the metronome to click on the "2" and "4" of each bar, or have it play on each "and" in a bar. There are a variety of ways to use the metronome. Use your imagination.

Accent Studies

8th notes with accents

This section combines alternate stickings with one-handed stickings, while stressing accents. It is essential to maintain only two dynamic levels in each exercise: the accented level and the unaccented level. Also, be sure to keep an even sound when moving from alternate strokes to one-handed strokes, and vice-versa. Following is a list of suggestions for different ways to play this section:

Play without accents—make sure each stick sounds the same, as though the exercise is being played with one hand.

Vary the dynamic level between the accented notes and the unaccented notes. For example: 1) unaccented notes *p*; accents *mf*. 2) unaccented notes *mf*; accents *f*. 3) unaccented notes *mp*; accents *ff*; etc.

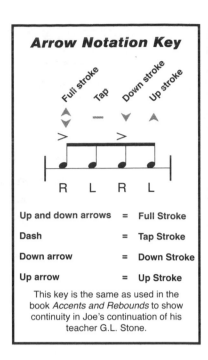

When one-handed stickings are used, fill in 16ths with the opposite hand.
For example:

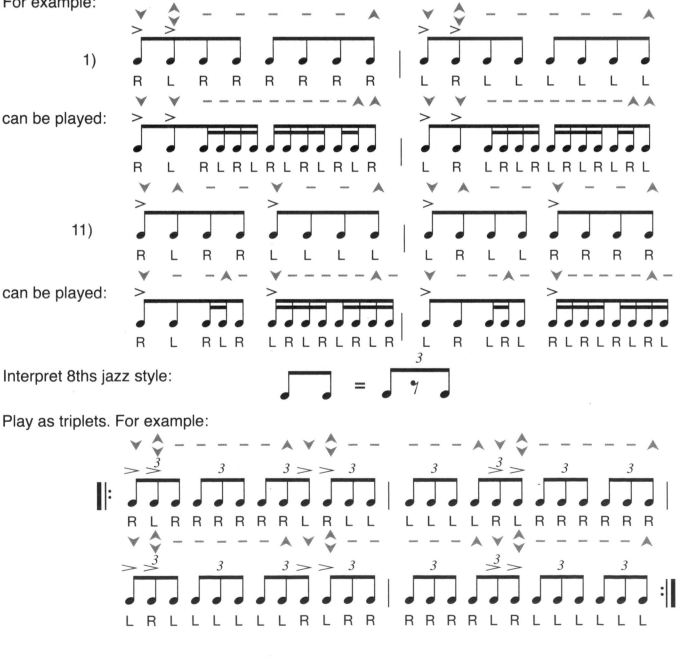

These exercises can also be applied to the drumset:

Play all previous suggestions while playing various patterns on bass drum and hi-hat. For example:

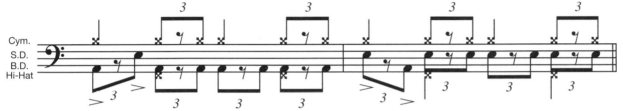

Play accented notes on tom-toms; unaccented notes on snare. Various patterns on bass and hi-hat.

Rights with right foot on bass drum; lefts with left hand on snare; right hand plays 8th notes on ride cymbal; hi-hat on "2" and "4".

Interpret 8ths jazz style; rights on bass; lefts on snare; jazz rhythm on ride cymbal; hi-hat on "2" and 4".

Play on double bass drums.

These are only a few of the many ways these exercises can be played. Try to find ways to apply these exercises to your own situation and your own needs.
Remember: these exercises only have value if they are applied in a musical way.

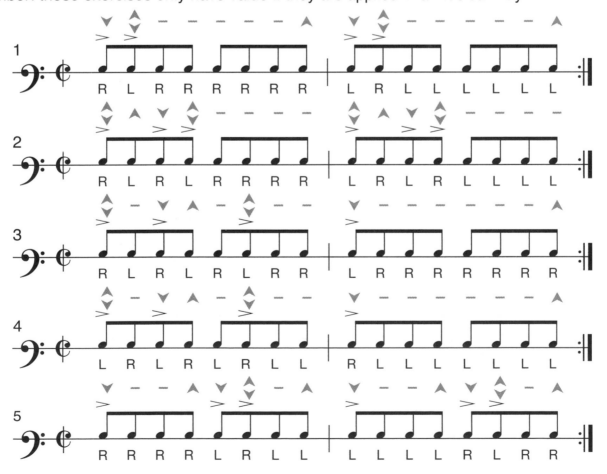

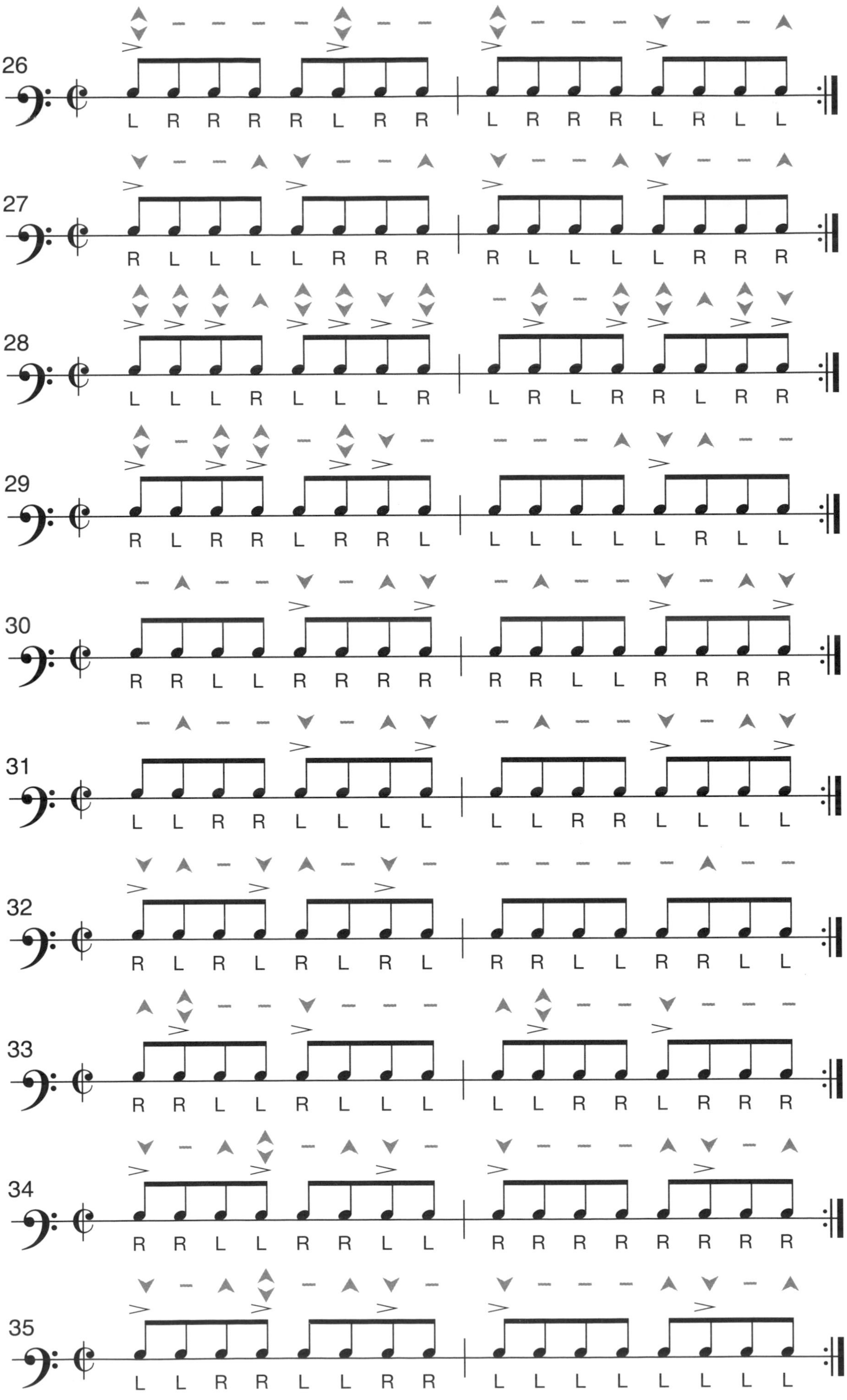
26
L R R R R L R R L R R R L R L L
27
R L L L L R R R R L L L L R R R
28
L L L R L L L R L R L R R L R R
29
R L R R L R R L L L L L L R L L
30
R R L L R R R R R R L L R R R R
31
L L R R L L L L L L R R L L L L
32
R L R L R L R L R R L L R R L L
33
R R L L R L L L L L R R L R R R
34
R R L L R R L L R R R R R R R R
35
L L R R L L R R L L L L L L L L

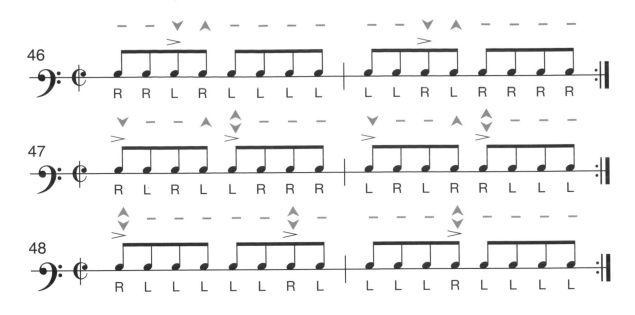

triplets with accents

This is similar to the first section, but here we're using triplets. Again, strive for evenness of sound, paying particular attention to the dynamic level between the accented and unaccented notes.

Many of the suggestions from the first section can be applied to this section as well. Here are some additional ideas:

Rights on bass drum; lefts on snare; hi-hat on "2" and "4"; shuffle rhythm on ride cymbal.

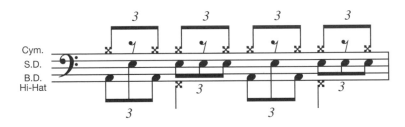

Play straight 8th notes on bass drum against the triplets (two against three).

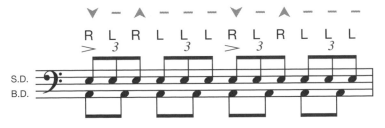

Transfer one-handed notes to bass drum.

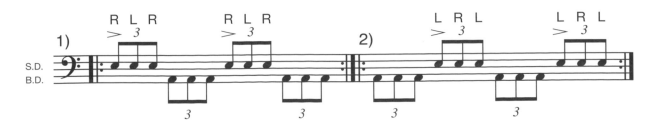

11
R L L R L L L R R L R R R L L R L L L R R L R R
12
R L R L R R L L L L L L L R L R L L R R R R R R
13
R L R L R L R R R R R R L R L R L R L L L L L L
14
R R R L R L R L R L L L R R R L R L R L R L L L
15
R R L L R R L L R R L L R R L L R R L L R R L L
16
R R R L L L R R R R R R L L L R R R L L L L L L
17
R R R R L R L L L L R L R R R R L R L L L L R L
18
R L L L L L L L R R L L R L L L L L L L R R L L
19
L R R R R R R R L L R R L R R R R R R R L L R R
20
R R R R L L L L R R R R L L L L R R R R L L L L

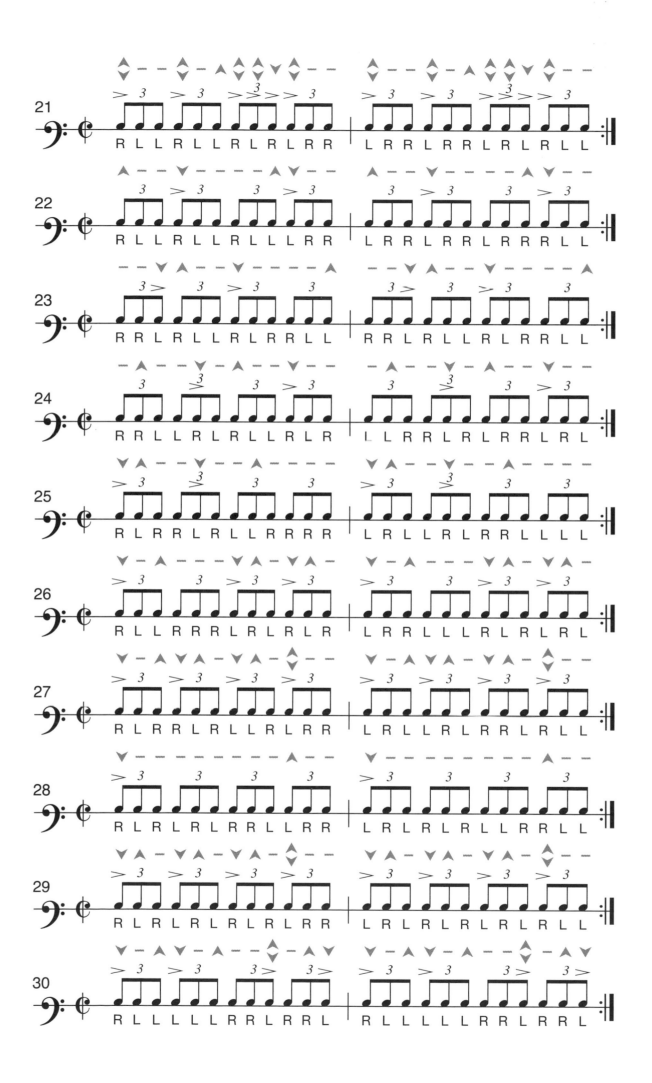

31
R L R L R L R R R L R R
L R L R L R L L L R L L
32
R L L L R R R L L L R R
R L L L R R R L L L R R
33
R L R L L R L L R L L R
L R L R R L R R L R R L
34
R R L R R L R L R L L R
L L R L R L R L R L R L
35
R R L L R L L R R L R R
L L R L L R R L R L R L
36
R L R L L R L R L R R L
R L R L L R L R L R R L
37
R L R L L L L L L L L L
L R L R R R R R R R R R
38
R L R L R L R R R R R R
L R L R L R L L L L L L
39
R L R L R L R L R L R L
L L L L L L R R R R R R
40
R L R L R L R L R L R L
R R R R R R R R R R R R

8th-note and triplet combinations

These exercises combine ideas from the previous two sections. Remember to pay attention to the *sound* you are making, and strive to eliminate any tension from your arms, wrists and fingers.

Buzz Roll Studies

8th notes with buzz rolls

Going from single strokes to buzz (multiple rebound) strokes requires a different pressure, which is controlled primarily with the fingers. The important thing to remember here is that "pressure" does not mean "rigidity" or "tension." So these exercises, then, will help develop the sensitivity in the fingers that is necessary to control this pressure. You must be able to immediately apply the pressure when needed for a buzz, and then be able to immediately release it for single strokes.

There are a variety of ways to play this section. Following are a few suggestions:

Play without accents.

Play the buzz notes as staccato as possible.

Play the buzz notes as legato as possible.

Play the buzz notes as double strokes.

Drumset suggestions:

Accent buzz strokes with the bass drum.

Play buzz notes on tom-toms, getting a muffled effect by pressing the stick into the head.

Play buzz notes on snare drum; all others on tom-toms.

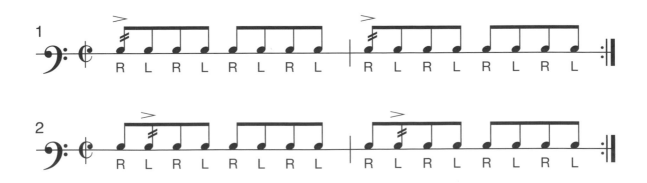

22

24

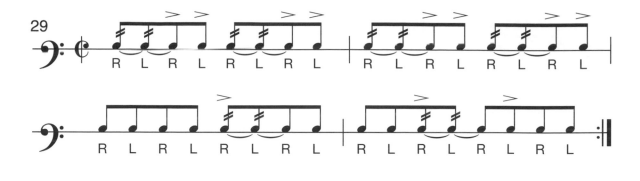

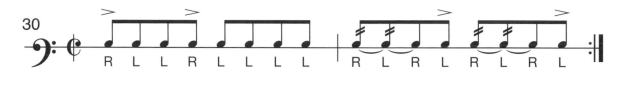

triplets with buzz rolls

These exercises are similar to those in the "8th Notes With Buzz Roll" section, in that they combine short buzzes with alternate or single-hand stickings. Remember to stay relaxed when changing pressure between single strokes and buzz notes.

26

28

Stroke Combination Studies

Going from single strokes to double strokes to buzz (multiple-rebound) strokes involves different pressures on the sticks. You must be able to change the pressure your fingers are putting on the sticks without tension developing in the wrists.

When going between single strokes and double strokes, the idea is to get the same sound, even though your hands are only moving half as fast when playing the doubles.

When moving between doubles and buzz strokes, the important thing is not to tighten up during the buzz notes. The hands will be moving at the same speed; the difference is the pressure you apply with your fingers.

When going from singles to buzz strokes, again, the hands will be going only half as fast on the bounce notes. The idea is to get as many rebounds as possible. Some people try to move their hands too fast because they're not getting enough rebounds. Practice slowly at first so you can concentrate on making the sticks rebound, even though at a slow tempo, the roll will not sound smooth. After you develop the ability to get a good rebound from the stick, you can increase the tempo and close the roll.

single and double combinations

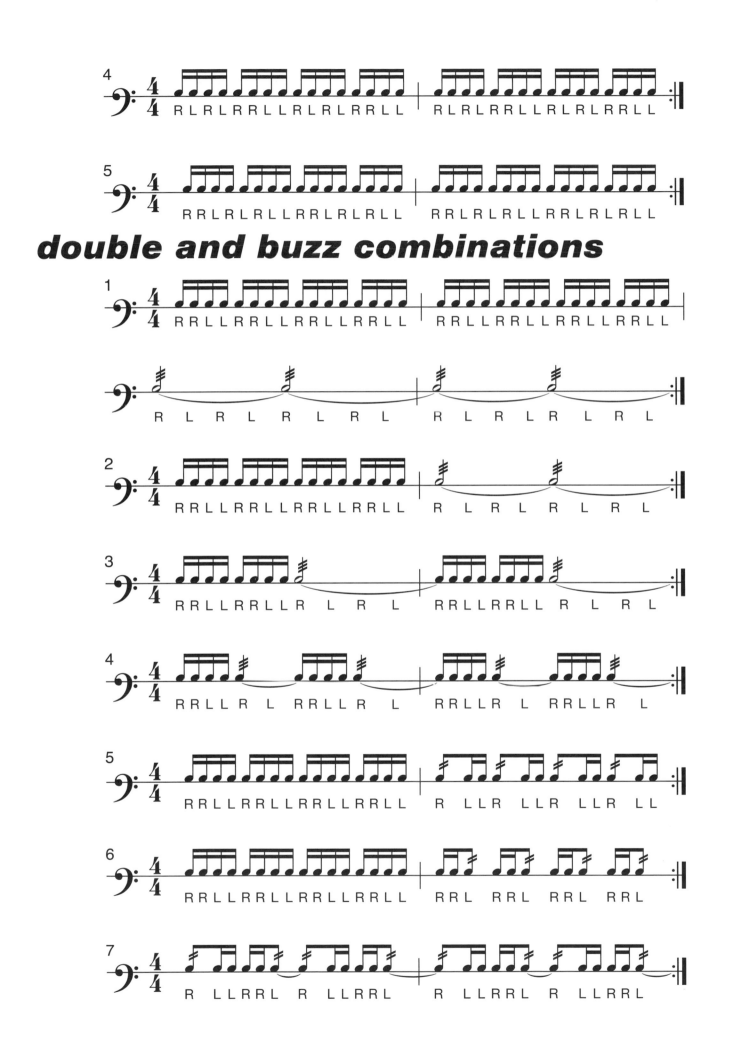

double and buzz combinations

single and buzz combinations

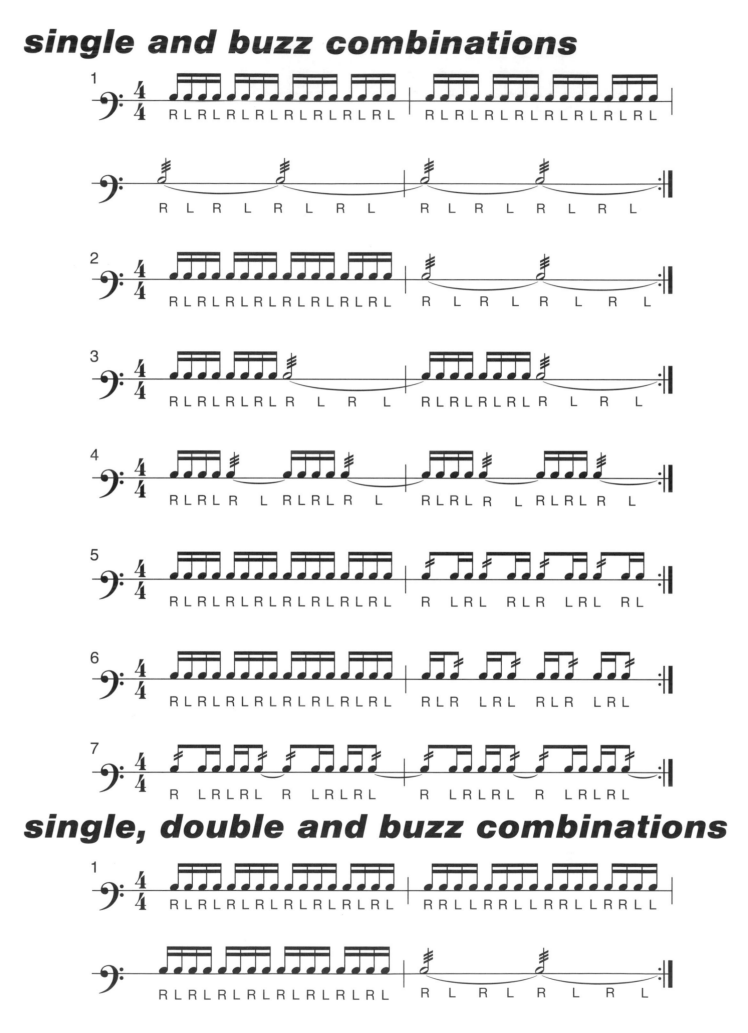

single, double and buzz combinations

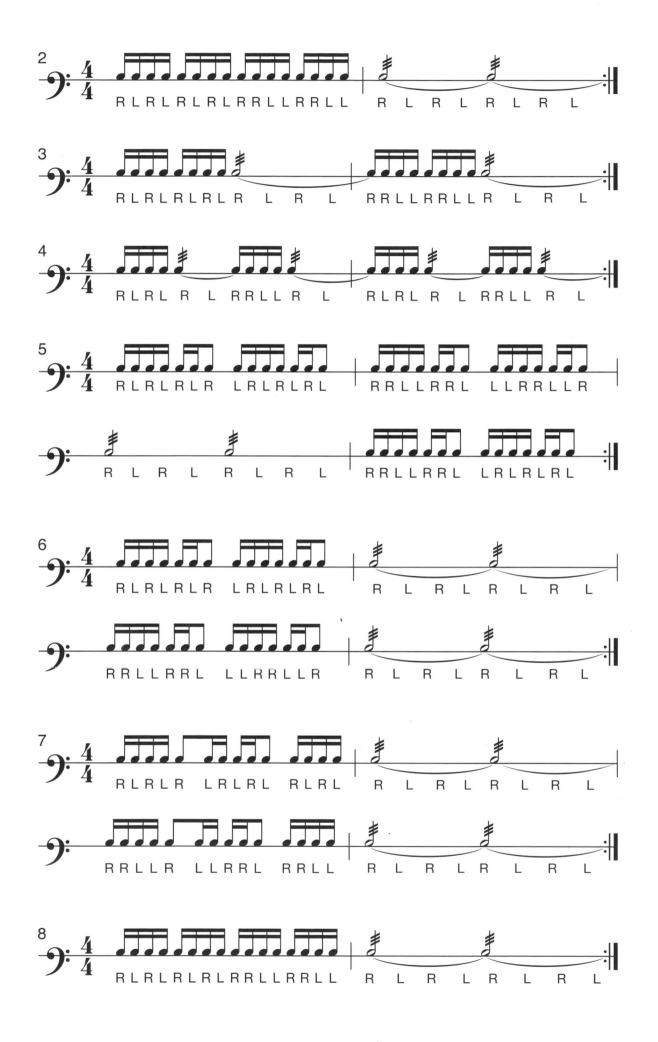

5-stroke roll combinations

7-stroke roll combinations

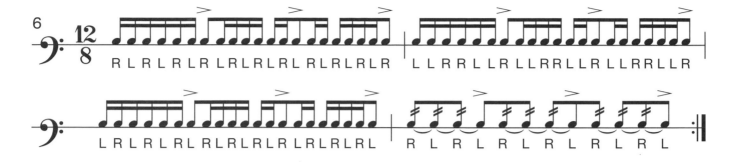

5-stroke and 7-stroke roll combinations

38

9-stroke roll combinations

Always remember that practicing these exercises merely for the technique is useless. You must apply the technique in a musical way.

Control Studies

sticking exercise

The purpose of these exercises is to develop the ability to go from one sticking to another, without changing the sound. In other words, each exercise should sound as though it is being played with one hand. You should start by practicing each exercise individually. After you reach a certain proficiency with each one, try playing them together, that is, going directly from the 8ths to the triplets, and then into the 16ths. Be sure that you do not tense up when you play the faster sections; you should be just as relaxed when playing the 16ths as you are when you play the 8ths.

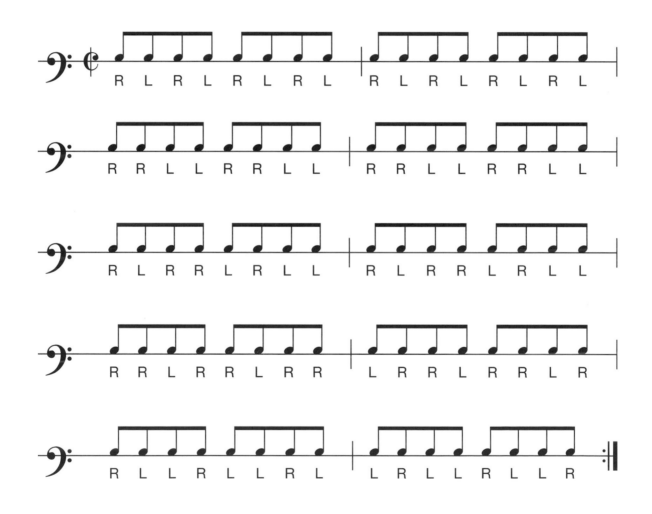

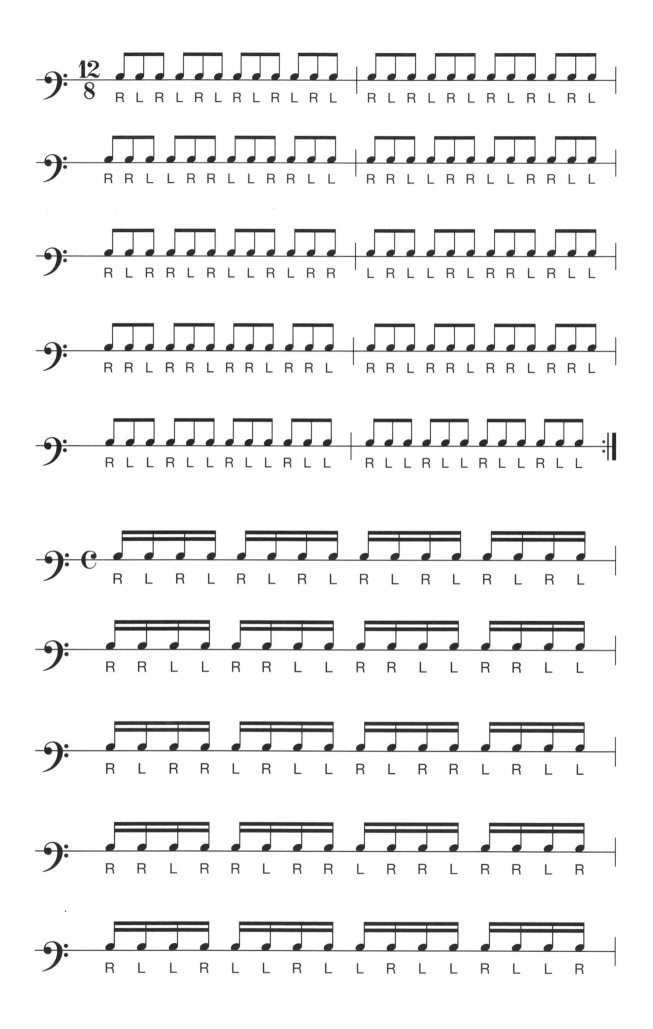

table of time

This will help your development of the single-stroke roll, and also help you develop the ability to play various subdivisions evenly. At first, you should accent the first note of each rhythmic grouping, as indicated. As proficiency increases, eliminate the accents.

Start the exercises slowly, at a metronome marking of about 53. As your technique and speed develop, increase the tempo setting on the metronome. Eventually, you should play this exercise at a marking of about 100. But start it slowly at first, making sure all the notes are even. Playing this smoothly and evenly is more important than playing it at a fast tempo. And *do* practice this with a metronome. (Refer to the section on "Using the Metronome" at the beginning of this book.)

Following are some suggestions to help you play the larger groupings.

Nine—This is based on the 8th note triplet. Think of dividing an 8th-note triplet into triplets.

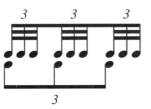

Ten—Based on the group of five. Play a five on each 8th-note beat, or think of playing a five grouping with the right hand, and filling in with the left.

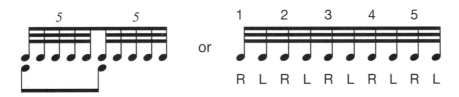

Eleven—This does not subdivide equally, but at first it might help you to count as shown.

Twelve—Play a six grouping on each 8th note count, or think of playing a six with the right hand while filling in with the left.

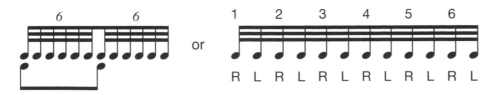

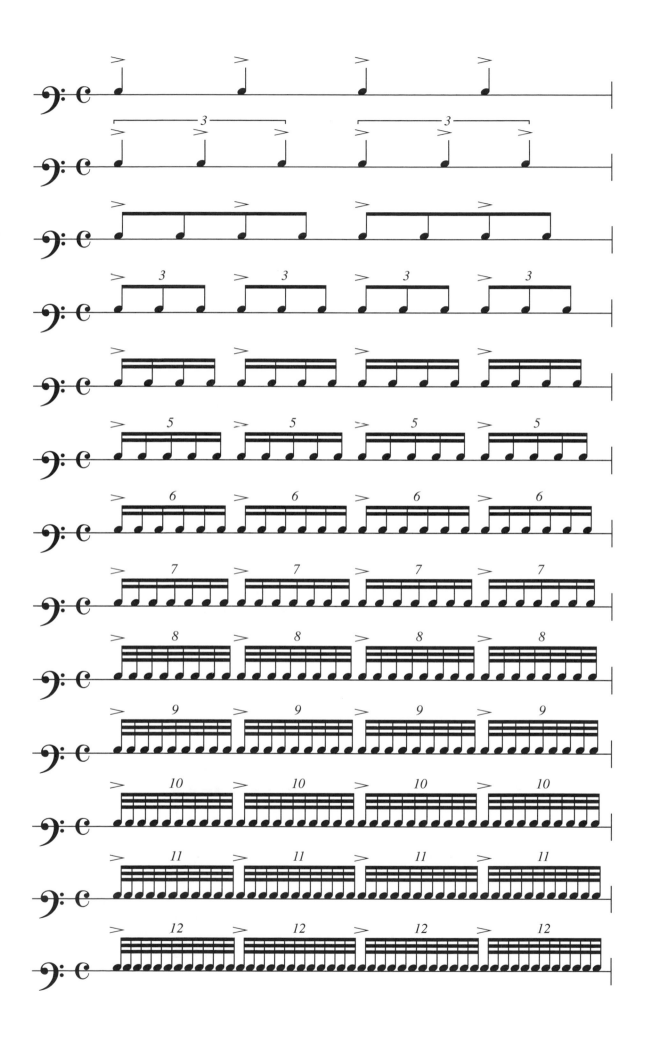

endurance

You should play each two-measure section four times before going on to the next line. As with the "Table of Time," start by accenting the first note of each rhythmic group. After you can do that easily, eliminate the accents.

Note: You may want to start out by just doing each line once. When you can do that comfortably, then increase to two times, then three, finally working your way up to doing each line four times. This is another good exercise to help develop your ability to play the single-stroke roll.

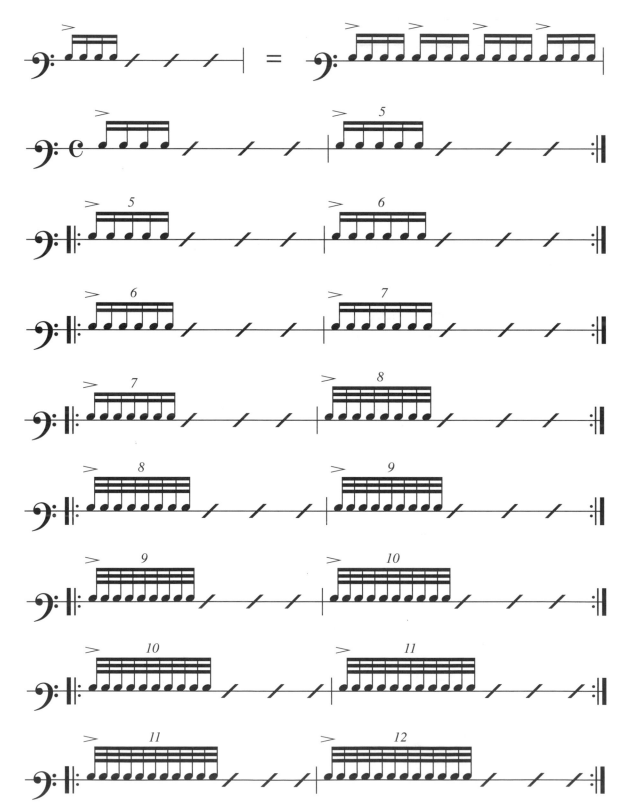

velocity

The faster you play, the looser and more relaxed you have to be. In these exercises, you just need to drop the stick and then keep it going. Try to get your hand to follow the motion of the stick. To do this, basically, the first note is struck using the wrist, and the other notes are controlled by the fingers. The important thing is to free yourself from tension, because any tension will break the flow of energy.

Practice each line eight times, slowly at first. Never play faster than a speed at which you can play relaxed and cleanly.

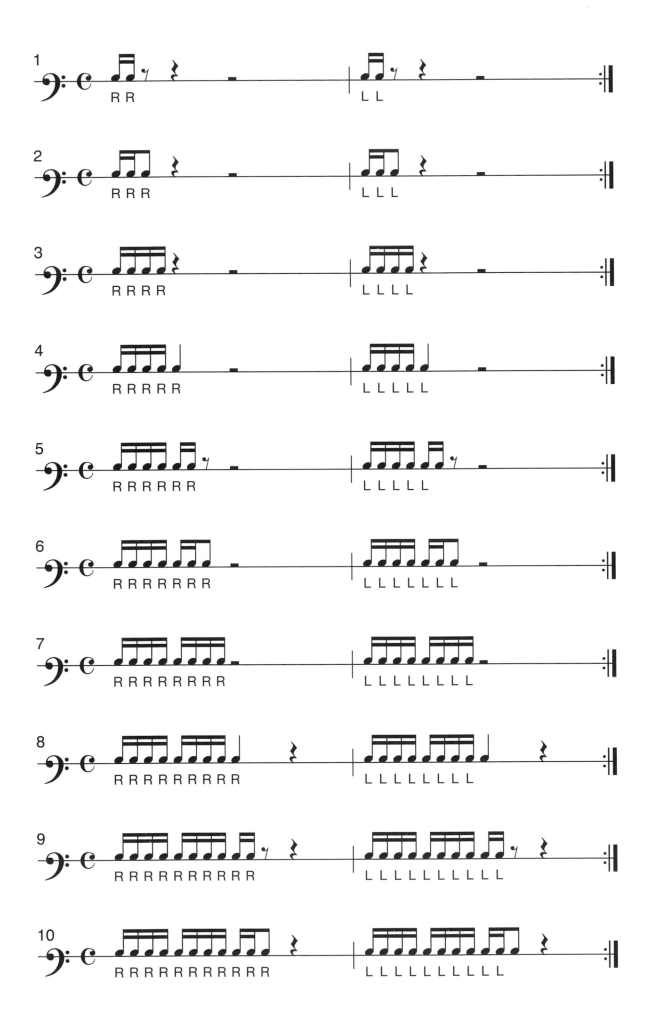

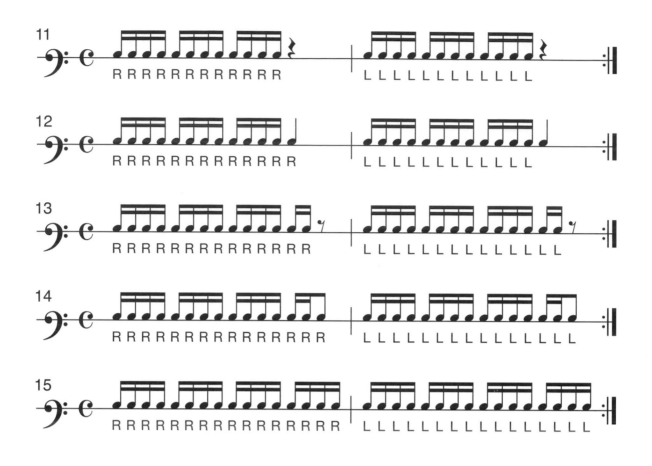

progressive accents

The idea of this is to give you the ability to accent anywhere in the bar that you want. I would suggest that you start by playing this *mf* and really hitting the accents hard (about *ff*). Play each bar eight times and then immediately go to the next bar until you have reached the end. After you are comfortable with this, practice with various dynamic levels, for example:

unaccented notes *p*; accents *mp*

unaccented notes *mp*; accents *fff*

unaccented notes *f*; accents *ff*, etc.

Another way to play these exercises is with accents on the first four 8th notes, throughout.

Practice these exercises using alternate sticking, starting with either hand.

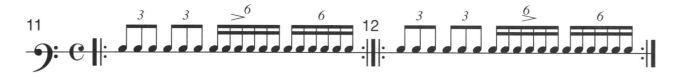

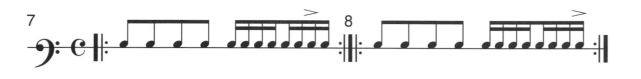

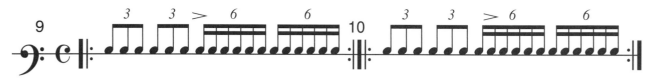

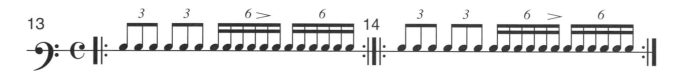

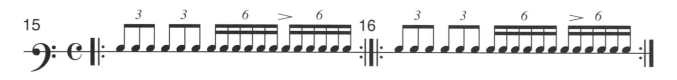

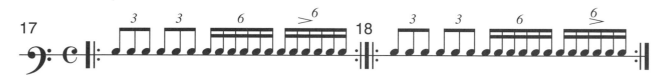

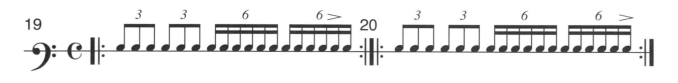

50

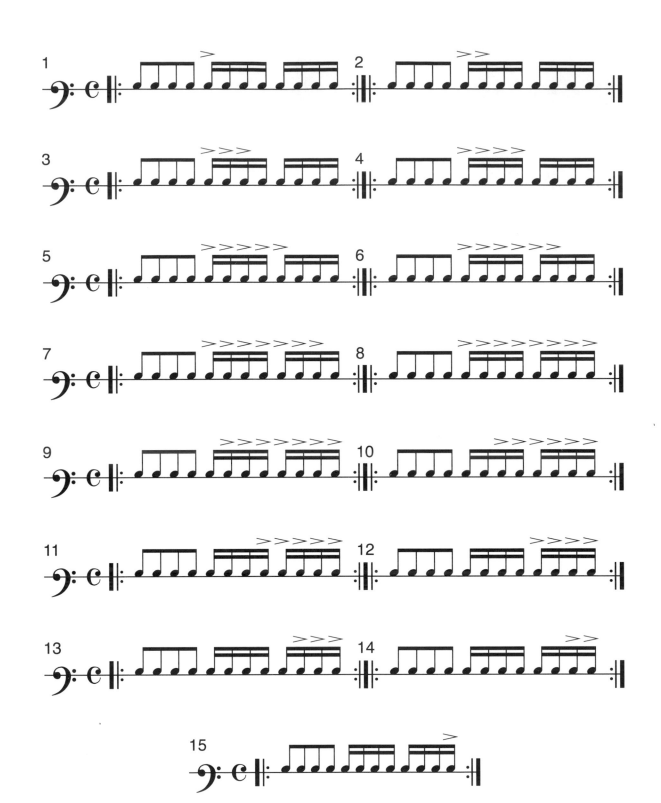

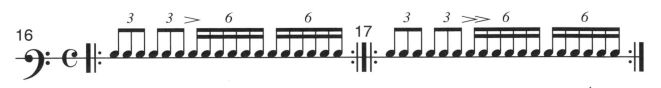

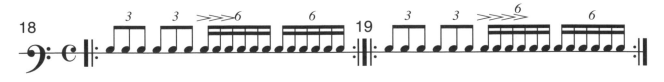

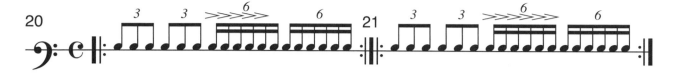

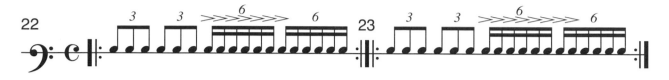

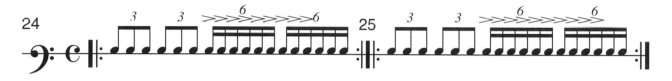

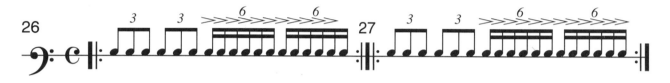

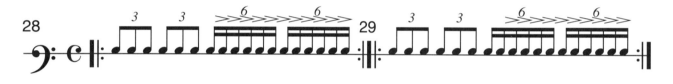

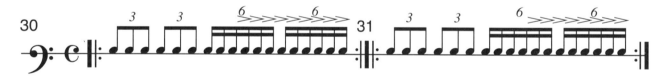

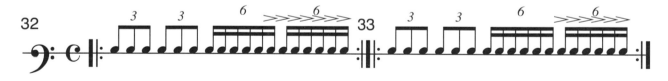

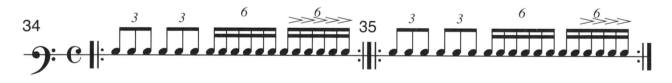

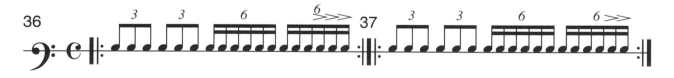

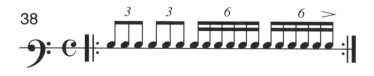

dynamics

These exercises are good for dynamic control, and they are also tremendous endurance builders. Within the crescendos and diminuendos, there should be no sudden changes in volume. They should be done smoothly so that with the crescendos, each note is louder than the one before, and with diminuendos, each note is softer than the one before. Take these slowly enough that you can control them.

Each exercise is written with a suggested dynamic range, but don't stop there. After mastering the range that is written, go back and apply a variety of dynamic ranges to the same exercises. For example, exercises 1 through 4 are written with a range from *pp* to *ff*. After practicing with that range, try the following suggestions: *ppp* to *fff*; pp to *mf*; mp to *ff*; *p* to *f*; and so on. The more ways you play these exercises, the more they will help you, and the more control you will gain.

the Stone "killer"

George Lawrence Stone wrote this out for me one day, and jokingly said, "This is a killer." I found it to be tremendous for endurance. Originally, he only wrote out the first four lines of this. I then expanded on it by adding accents and fill-ins, and then applying the same idea to triplets and duples. The idea, as Stone explained it, was to work each hand individually before you put them together. (Billy Gladstone used this same concept of developing each hand individually.)

These exercises are not meant to be practiced all at once. They are grouped into sections. First, start with the 8th-note section—the 4's, 8's, 12's and 16's. Play the 4's fifty times each (counting the right hand). Then do the 8's fifty times, the 12's fifty times, and the 16's fifty times. The first time you try this, you may not be able to do that many repetitions. If necessary, start by doing each line only ten times. Gradually work your way up to where you can do fifty repetitions. It may take several weeks; that's okay. Work at your own pace, depending on your stage of development. But remember: stay relaxed throughout the entire exercise. The key to speed and endurance is relaxation. Do not allow yourself to tense up in an attempt to play faster or longer. As soon as you become tense, you are defeating the purpose of the exercise.

After you have reached a certain proficiency with the first section, go to the section with the accents on the first note of each group. Practice this the same way as the first section—gradually working your way up to more repetitions. At this point, It would be good to continue practicing the first section In addition to the second section.

After reaching a proficiency with the second section, move to the third section—accents on the last note of each group. At this point, you might stop working on the first section and concentrate only on the two sections with accents.

Once you feel fairly comfortable with the accent sections, move on to the section with fill-ins. Again, start with only as many repetitions as you can handle comfortably. (Although by now, after having spent a few weeks with the first three sections, you should be seeing an obvious improvement in your endurance.) Practice the fill-in sections in the same manner in which you practiced the first three sections: work on the unaccented section first, and then add the accented sections.

Once you have worked your way through all six sections, you can move on to the triplet exercises, and then the duple exercises.

Stone "killer" : part one

Section 1

Section 2

56

Section 3

Section 4

Section 5

Section 6

Stone "killer" : part two

Section 1

Section 2

Section 3

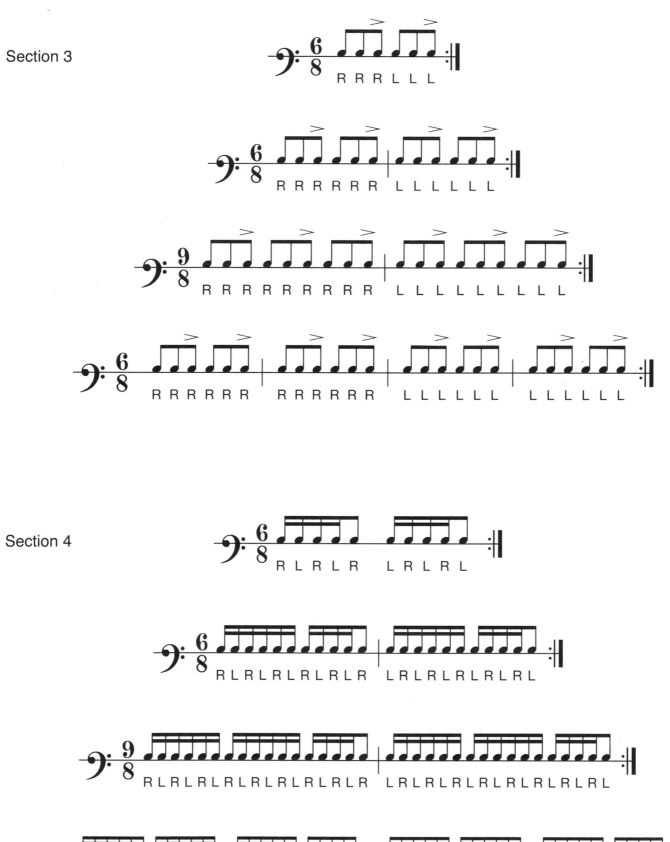

Section 4

60

Section 5

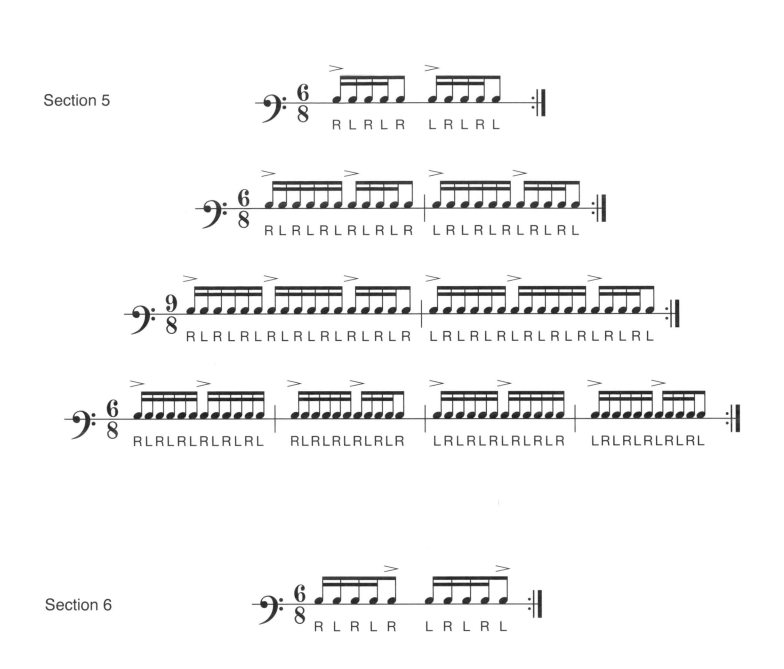

Section 6

Stone "killer" : part three

Section 1

Section 2

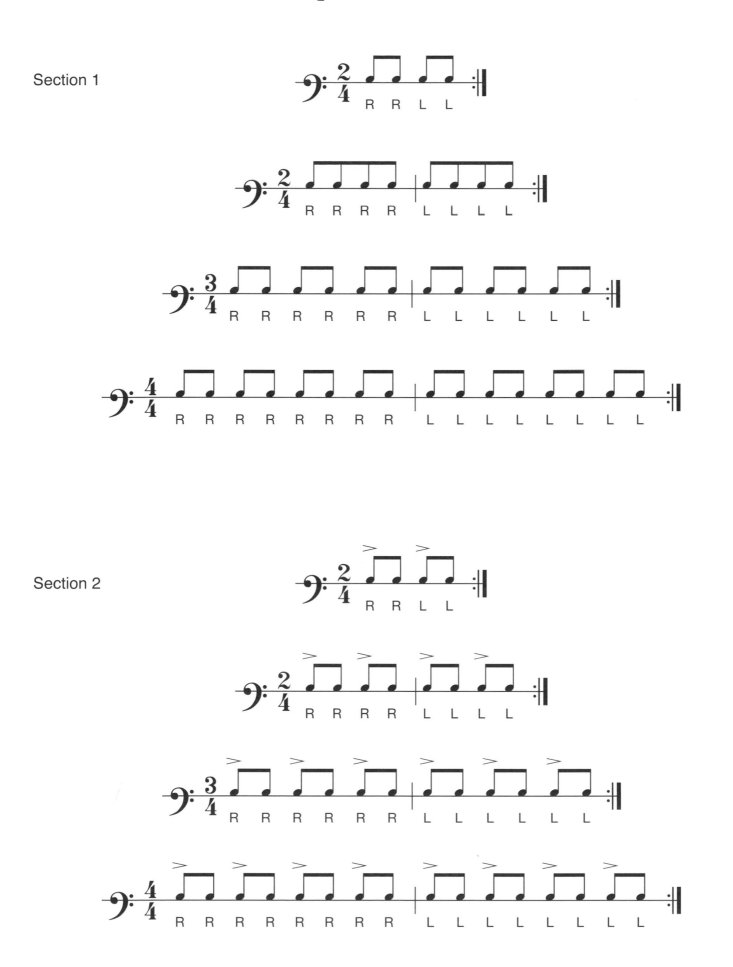

62

Section 3

Section 4

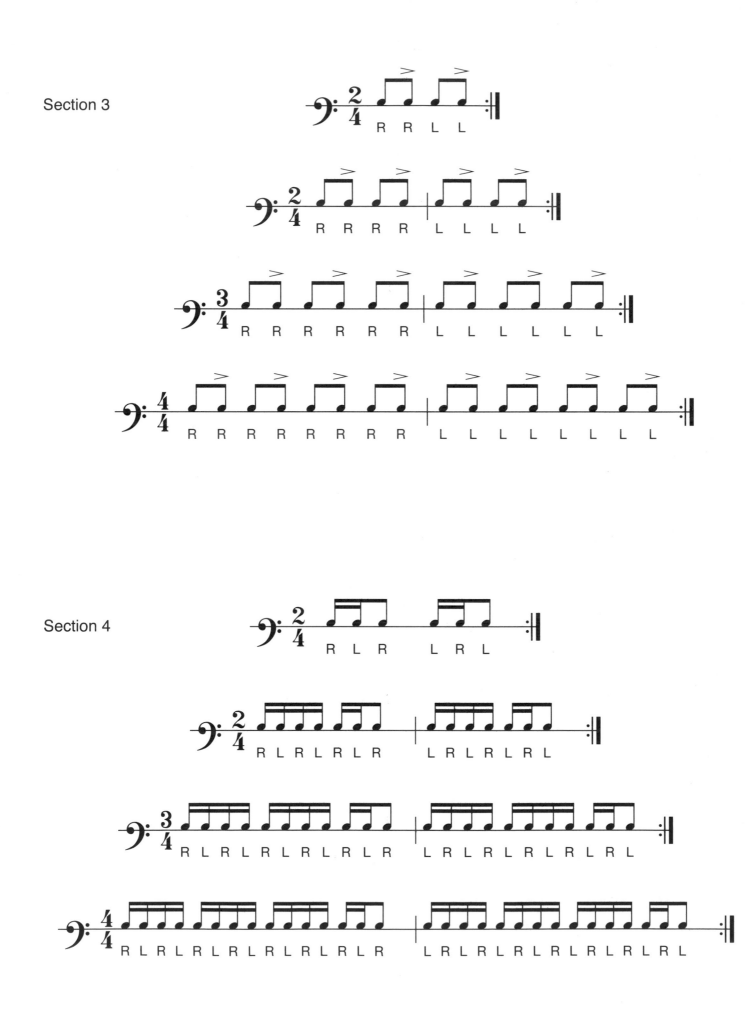

Section 5

Section 6

64

Eventually you can practice various combinations of exercises. A few suggestions are given below.

The "Stone Killer" can also be applied to drumset. Here are some suggestions:

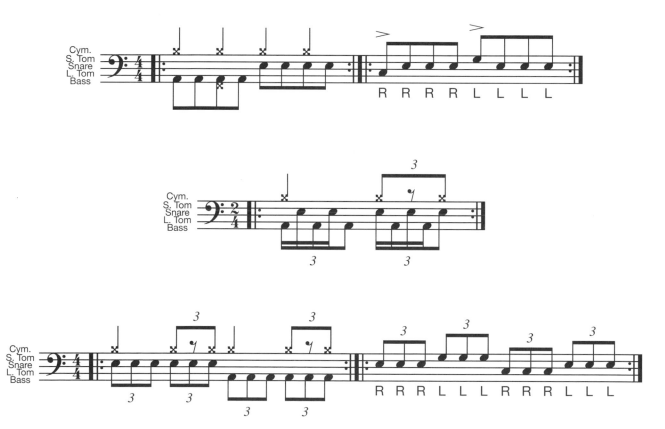

Remember to always use your own imagination to come up with additional ways to use these exercises.

Fill-In Studies

groups of three with fill-ins

The idea of this is to keep a continuous flow of accented triplets with one hand, while filling in with the other hand. This, again, goes back to the principle of developing each hand individually. It will also help develop your ability to accent, and doing the fill-ins will help your coordination. These exercises are written with a left-hand lead, but you should also practice these with a right-hand lead—accented triplets with the right hand; fill-ins with the left hand.

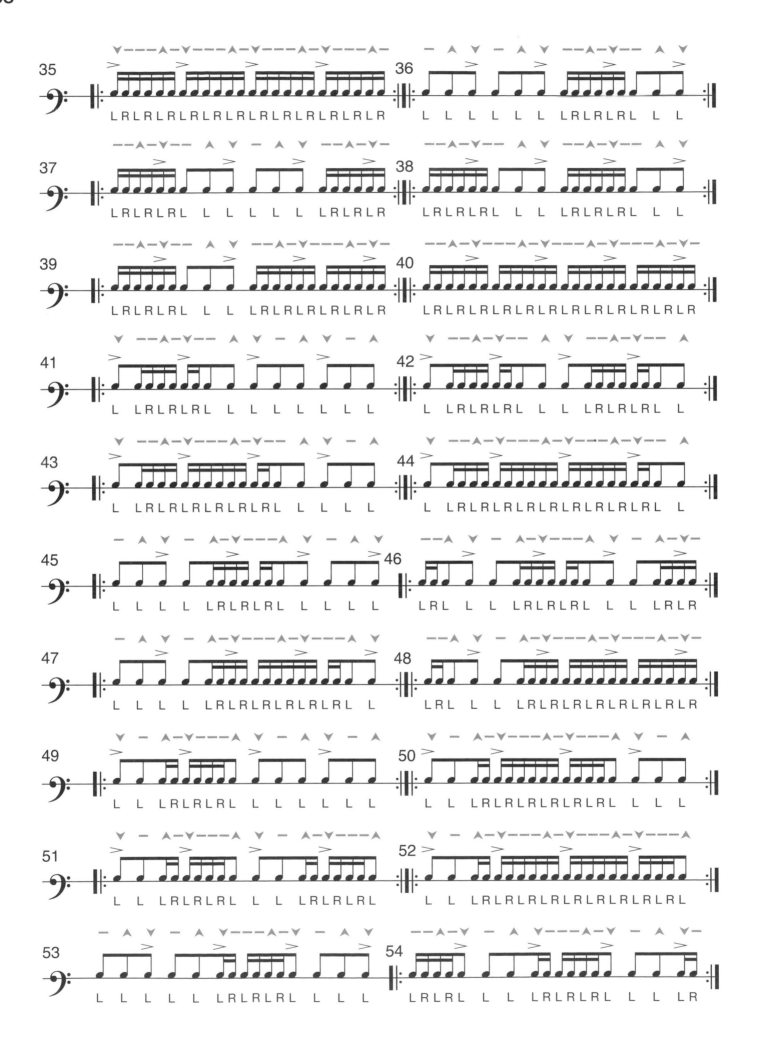

69

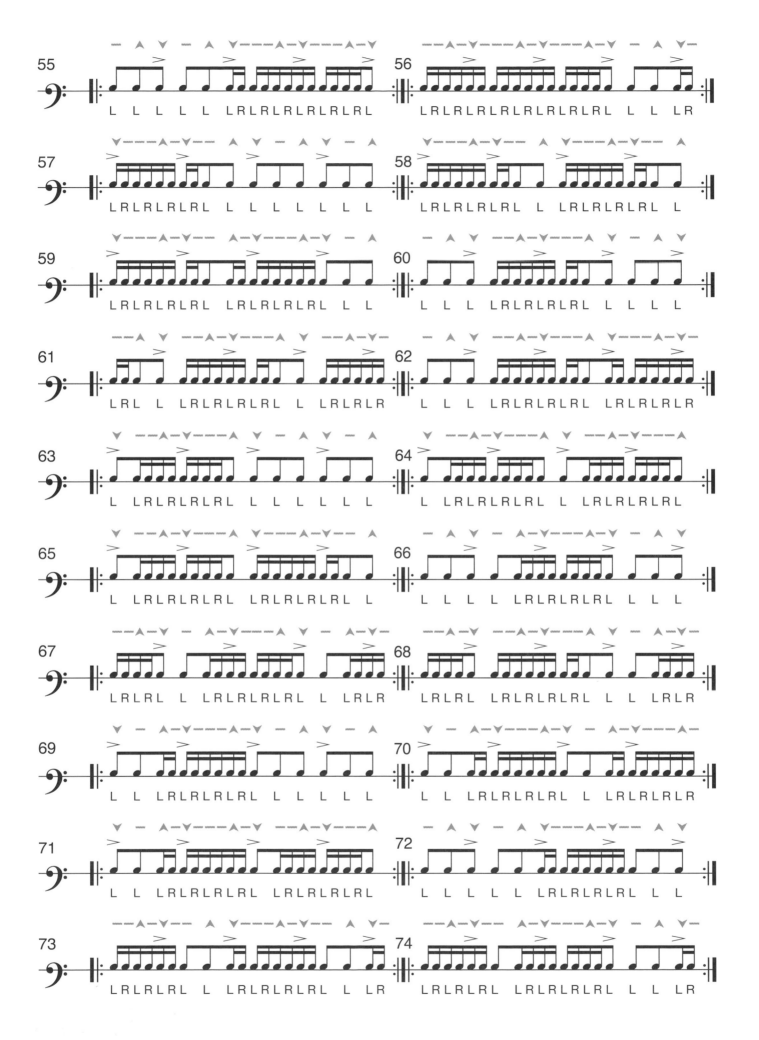

groups of four with fill-ins

This is based on the same idea as the previous section. Here, you will be playing accented groups of four with one hand, while filling in with the other hand. Again, after learning to play these as written, you should practice them with the stickings reversed.

threes and fours with fill-ins

This is based on a combination of the previous two sections. It is recommended that you practice each of these first without the fill-in notes. For example, number 1 should first be practiced like this:

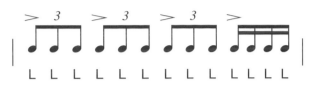

Remember to practice these examples with the stickings reversed.

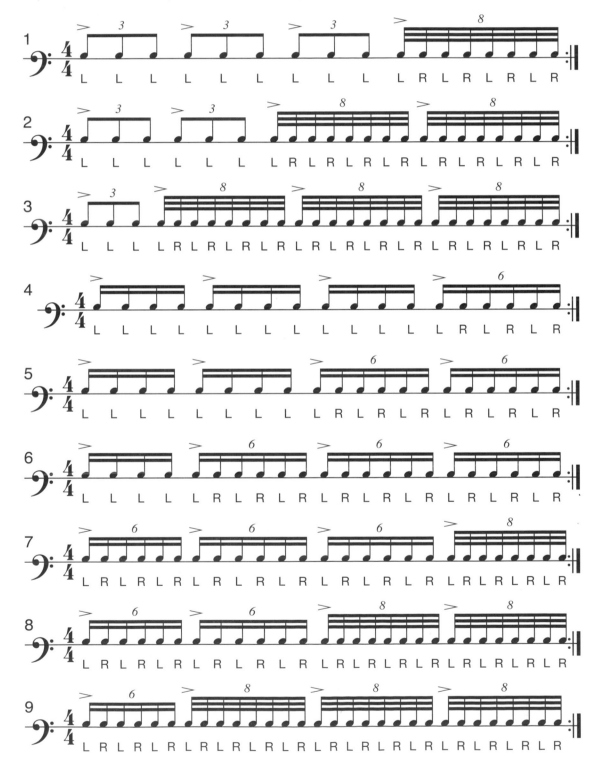

groups of two with fill-ins

This section is based on playing accented groups of two with one hand, while filling in with the other hand. As with the previous sections, practice these also with a right-hand lead.

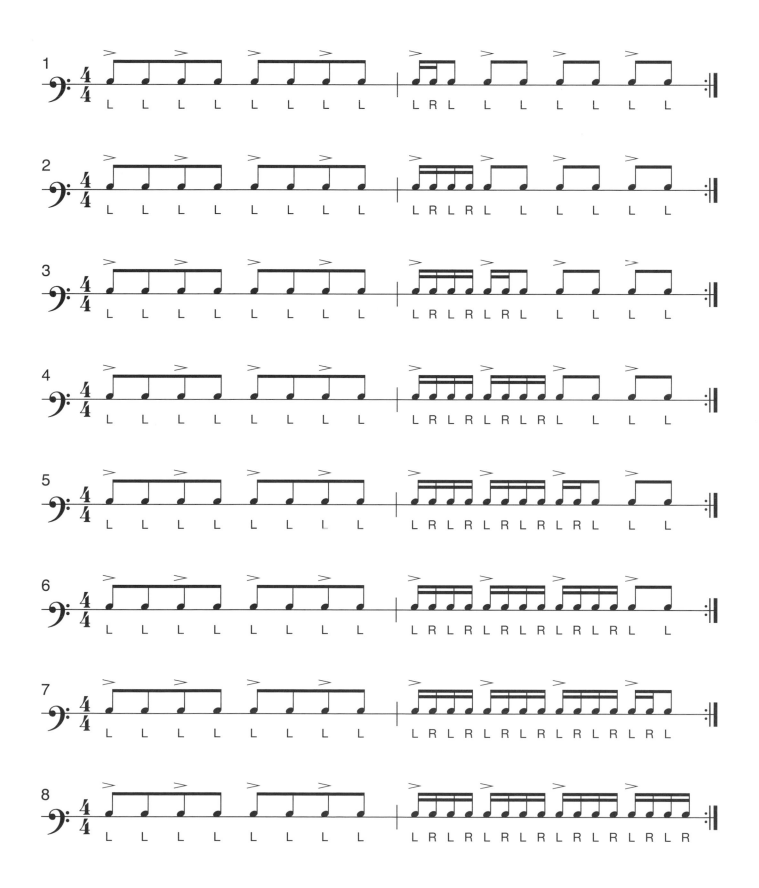

74

endurance exercise with fill-ins

This exercise should also be practiced starting with the right hand. Start slowly and gradually work it up. Each line should be played eight times.

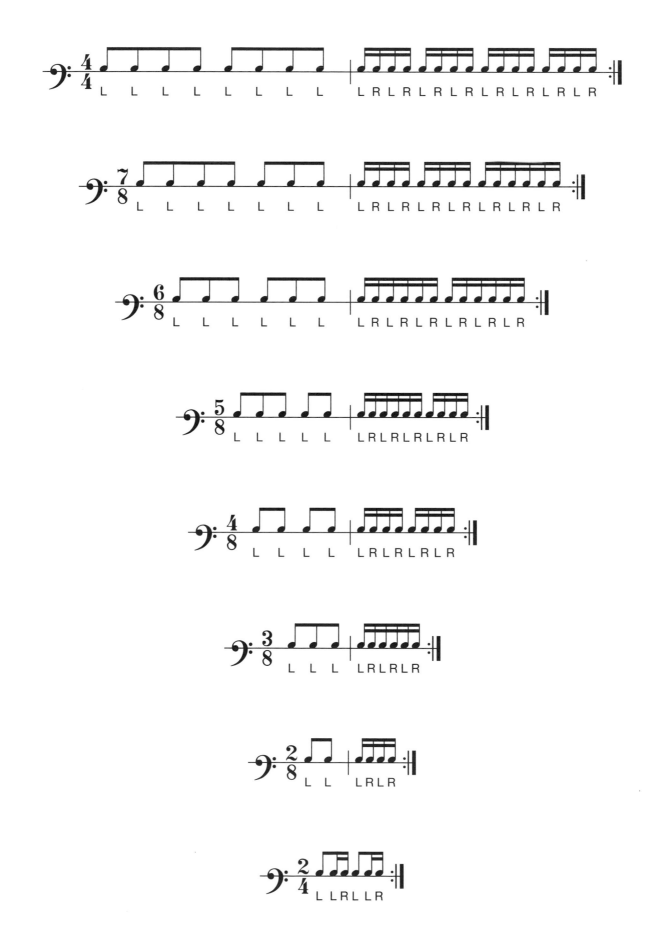

Ostinato Studies

Note: Before studying this section, you should be proficient with the "Stone Killer" section.

The idea here is to be able to play an ostinato with one hand and have total freedom with the other hand. Again, we're dealing with control of the instrument. The more control you have, the more confident you will be as a player.

You should first practice each ostinato figure by itself, using only the left hand. Then practice each one using only the right hand. (This goes back to the idea of developing each hand individually and then putting them together. Practicing these exercises in this way will also be good for accent control.)

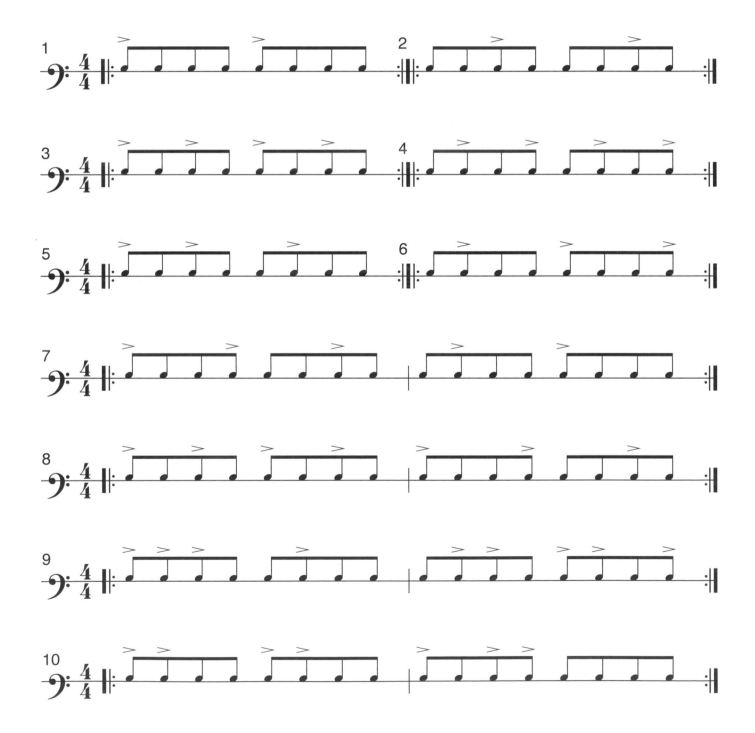

Note: this is merely an accent played on every third note.

After practicing these patterns, the patterns given in the "8th Notes With Accents" section and the "8th-Note Triplets With Accents" section of this book can also be used as ostinatos by playing each example with one hand.

After you feel comfortable with an ostinato pattern, play the pattern with your left
hand, while playing different rhythms with your right. A few examples are given
to get you started, but don't stop with those. Learn to play any possible rhythm
against the ostinato. After you can do this, reverse hands: play the ostinato with
the right hand and the various rhythms with the left.

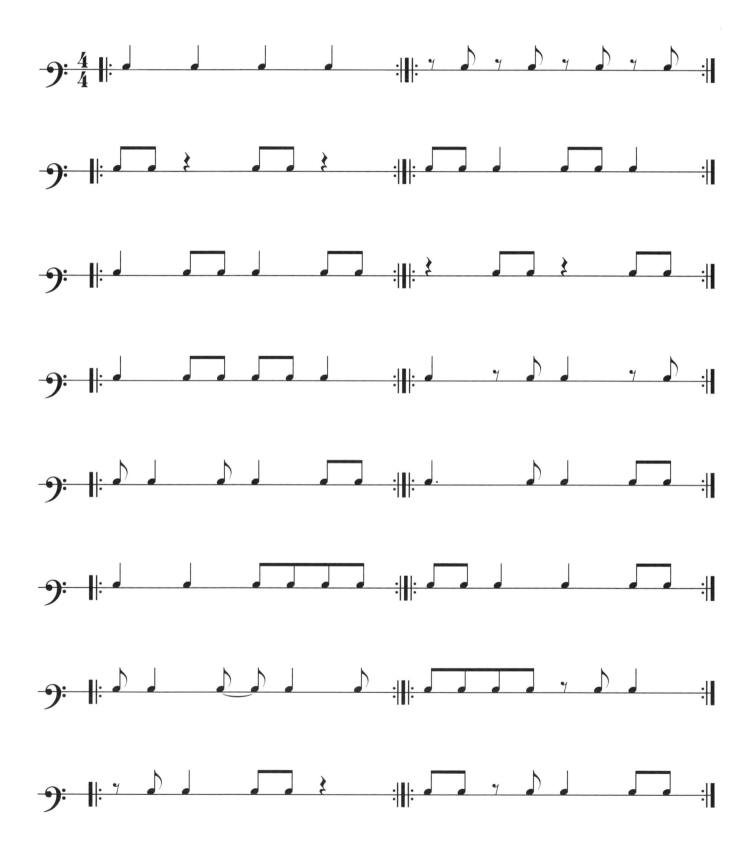

These patterns, obviously, are only to get you started. Alter you can play each
of these in conjunction with an ostinato, practice additional patterns of your own
choice, until you are able to play any possible rhythm with one hand, while maintaining an ostinato with the other. You should also apply various accents and
dynamics to these patterns.

Once you have reached a certain proficiency, start putting the rhythms together into phrases. An eight-measure example is given, but again, don't stop here. Take any reading book and play the music against an ostinato. Also, the "Flat Flams" section in this book can be adapted to ostinato playing. The ultimate is to be able to improvise freely with one hand, while playing an ostinato with the other.

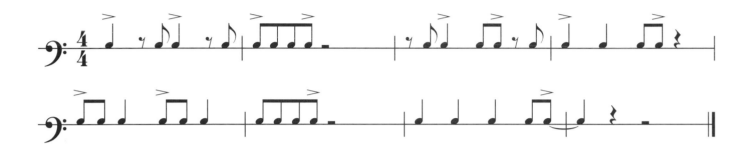

Following are a few suggestions for using ostinatos on the drumset:

Ostinato with left hand on snare; improvise freely with right hand on cymbals or tom-toms.

Same as above with various bass drum and hi-hat patterns.

Ostinato with left hand on snare or closed hi-hat; various rhythms broken up between right hand on tom-toms and right foot on bass drum.

Ostinato with right hand on floor tom; left hand improvising freely on snare drum.

Ostinato with right hand on bell of ride cymbal; different ostinato with left hand on snare drum.

The possibilities for using ostinatos are limited only by your own imagination. Be creative.

Note: the author used this idea on "Bossa Nova U.S.A." with the Dave Brubeck Quartet. A bossa nova pattern was played as an ostinato on the snare drum with the left hand, and the right hand freely improvised on the ride cymbal.

82

Flam Studies

flat flams

The term "flat flam" is used here to describe both sticks hitting exactly together. These exercises are most effective when played on two different surfaces. They could be played on two different drums, a drum and a cymbal, a drum and a cow-bell, or whatever. One hand is maintaining a steady pulse (first 8th notes, then 8th-note triplets) while the other hand plays various rhythms. After learning to do these with the hands, they could also be done with the feet, or with combinations of hands and feet. Use your imagination.

8th notes with flams

These exercises should first be played as written, on a snare drum or practice pad, without accenting the flams. After playing these at a medium dynamic, practice at various dynamic levels, from very soft to very loud. You should also practice different ways of playing the flams, from very closed—almost "flat"—to somewhat open. As with any exercise, adapt it to your own particular needs, and to the type of music you will be playing. A rudimental drummer will probably use a lot of arm motion in playing the flams; a concert drummer might want to work on these using finger and wrist control; a drumset player might want to play the flams between different drums. Use your Imagination. These examples are only to give you ideas.

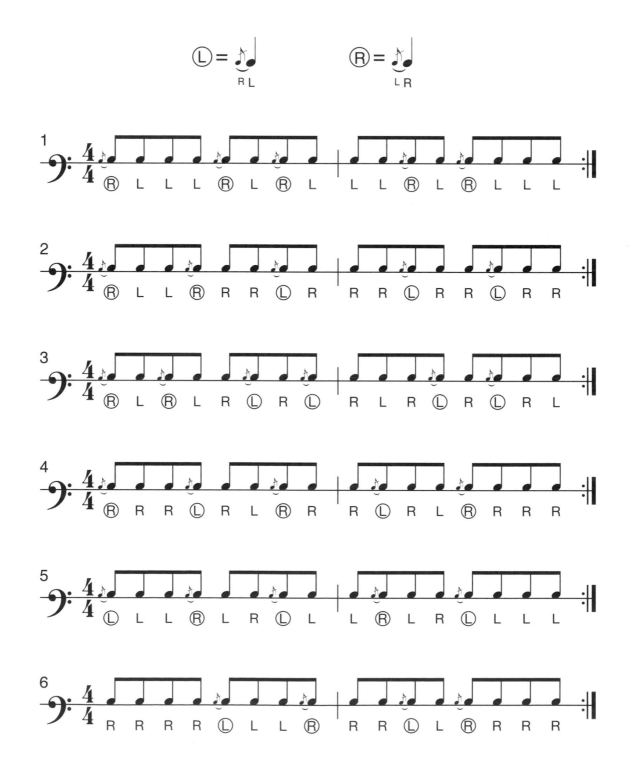

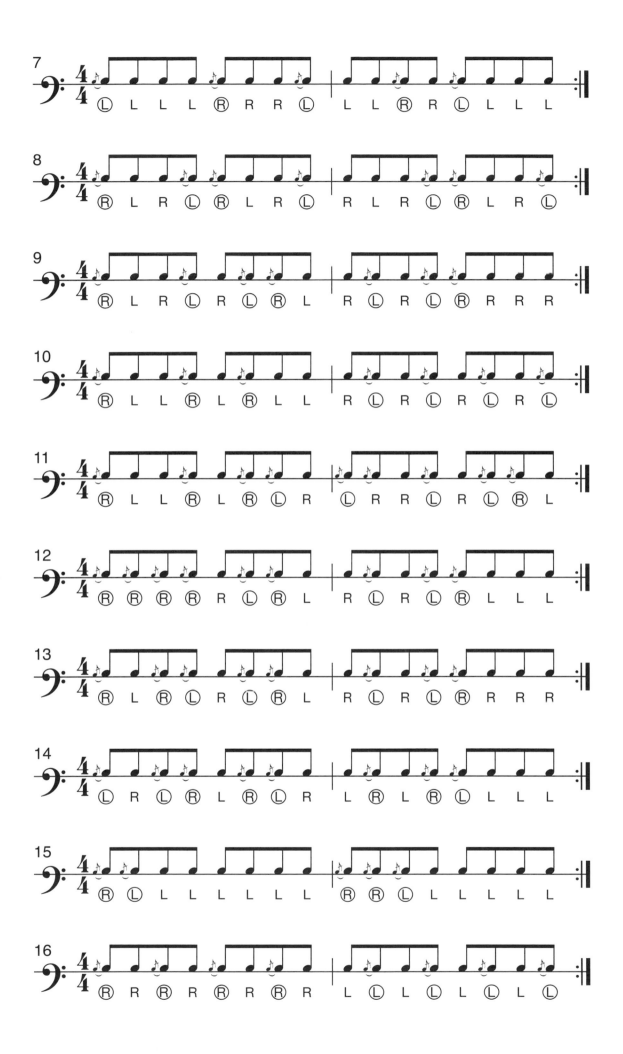

88

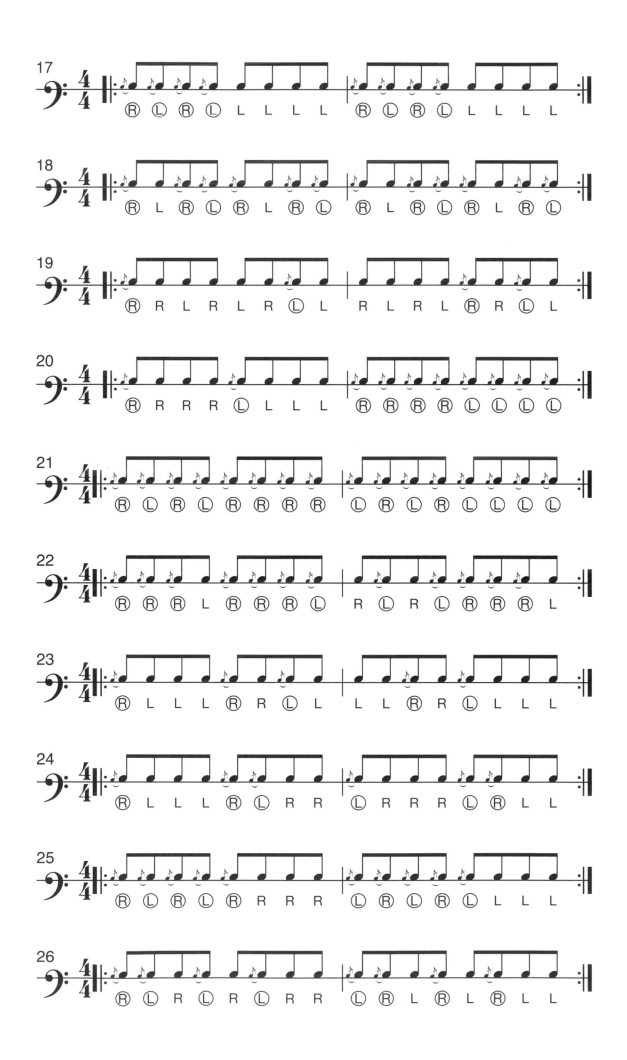

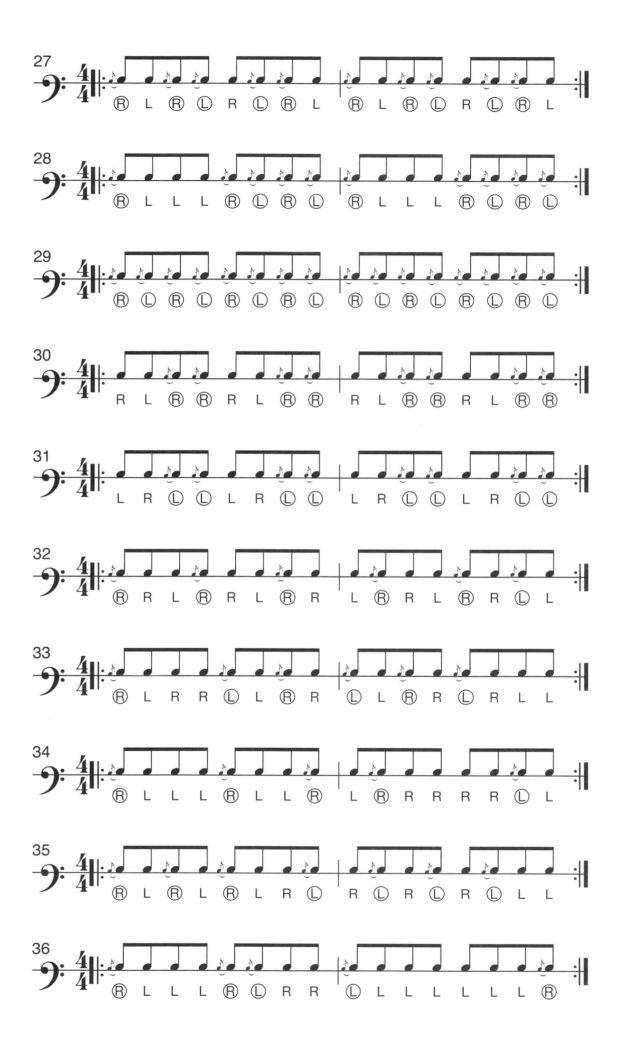

triplets with flams

20
Ⓡ L R Ⓛ R L R L Ⓡ L R Ⓛ Ⓡ L R Ⓛ R L R L Ⓡ L R Ⓛ
21
Ⓡ R R R R R R R Ⓛ R R R Ⓛ L L L L L L L Ⓡ L L L
22
Ⓡ L R R Ⓛ R L L Ⓡ L R R Ⓛ R L L Ⓡ L R R Ⓛ R L L
23
R R Ⓛ R L L Ⓡ L Ⓡ R Ⓛ L Ⓡ R Ⓛ L Ⓡ R Ⓛ R L Ⓡ L L
24
Ⓡ L R R R R Ⓛ R Ⓛ R Ⓛ R Ⓛ R L L L L Ⓡ L Ⓡ L Ⓡ L
25
Ⓡ R L R L R Ⓛ L R L R L Ⓡ R L R L R Ⓛ L R L R L
26
Ⓡ R L Ⓡ R L Ⓛ L R Ⓛ L R Ⓡ R L Ⓡ R L Ⓛ L R Ⓛ L R
27
Ⓡ L R Ⓛ L R Ⓛ R L Ⓡ R L Ⓡ L R Ⓛ L R Ⓛ R L Ⓡ R L
28
Ⓡ R R Ⓛ L R Ⓛ L L Ⓡ R L Ⓡ R R Ⓛ L R Ⓛ L L Ⓡ R L
29
Ⓡ L R Ⓛ R L ⓇⓁⓇⓁⓇⓁ Ⓡ L R Ⓛ R L ⓇⓁⓇⓁⓇⓁ

These patterns are not necessarily the ones you will use when playing, but you will be able to use the same techniques any way you want. You may be able to hear a million "hip" phrases in your mind, but If you can't get them out, they won't do you any good. So this is to give you the facility to play what you hear in your mind. These exercises may also stimulate your imagination, which will, in turn, develop your own creativity.

Biography

Joe Morello was born on July 17, 1929. in Springfield Mass. Having impaired vision since birth, he devoted himself to indoor activities. At the age of six, his family's encouragement led him to studying the violin. Three years later, he was featured with the Boston Symphony Orchestra as soloist in the Mendelssohn Violin Concerto. At the age of twelve, he made a second solo appearance with this orchestra. But upon meeting and hearing his idol, the great Heifitz, Joe felt he could never achieve "that sound." So at the age of fifteen, Joe changed the course of his musical endeavors and began to study drums

Joe's first drum teacher, Joe Sefcik, was a pit drummer for all of the shows in the Springfield area. He was an excellent teacher and gave Joe much encouragement. Joe began sitting in with any group that would allow it. When he was not sitting in, he and his friends, including Teddy Cohen, Chuck Andrus, Hal Sera, Phil Woods, and Sal Salvador, would get together and jam in any place they could find. Joe would play

any job he was called for. As a result, his musical experiences ranged from rudimental military playing to weddings and social occasions. Eventually, Mr. Sefcik decided it was time for Joe to move on. He recommended a teacher In Boston, the great George Lawrence Stone.

Mr. Stone did many things for Joe. He gave Joe most of the tools for developing technique. He taught Joe to read. But probably most important of all, he made Joe realize his future was in jazz, not legitimate percussion as Joe had hoped. Through his studies with Mr. Stone, Joe became known as the best drummer in Springfield, and rudimental champion of New England.

Joe's playing activity increased, and he soon found himself on the road with several groups. First there was Hank Garland and the Grand Old Opry, and then Whitey Bernard. After much consideration, Joe left Whitey Bernard to go to New York City.

A difficult year followed, but with Joe's determination and

Joe Morello with George Lawrence Stone.

Joe during his early years in New York.

The Dave Brubeck Quartet performing at the White House.

the help of friends like Sal Salvador, Joe began to be noticed. Soon he found himself playing with an impressive cast of musicians that included Gil Melle, Johnny Smith, Tal Farrow, Jimmy Raney, Stan Kenton, and Marian McPartland. After leaving Marian McPartland's trio, he turned down offers from the Benny Goodman band and the Tommy Dorsey band. The offer he chose to accept was a two-month temporary tour with the Dave Brubeck Quartet, which ended up lasting twelve-and-a-half years. It was during this period that Joe's technique received its finishing touches from Billy Gladstone of Radio City Music Hall.

Since 1968, when the Dave Brubeck Quartet disbanded, Joe has spread his talents over a variety of areas. He maintains a very active private teaching practice. Through his association with the Ludwig Drum Company, Joe has made great educational contributions to drumming, as well as the entire field of jazz, by way of his clinics, lectures and guest solo appearances. With the help of his guide dog, Matthew, Joe has been performing with his own group throughout the United States.

Joe has appeared on over 120 albums, of which 60 were with the Dave Brubeck Quartet. He won the *down beat* award for five years in a row, the *Playboy* award for seven years in a row, and is the only drummer to win every music poll for five years in a row, including Japan, England, Europe, Australia, and South America. He is mentioned in *Who's Who in the East*, twelfth edition, and the *Blue Book*, which is a listing of persons In the United Kingdom, Ireland, Canada, Australia, New Zealand, and the United States who have achieved distinction in the arts, sciences, business, or the professions. Revered by fans and musicians alike, Joe is considered to be one of the finest, and is probably one of the most celebrated, drummers In the history of jazz.

MODERN DRUMMER® Media
Presents: Lessons From The Greats

The Joe Morello Collection

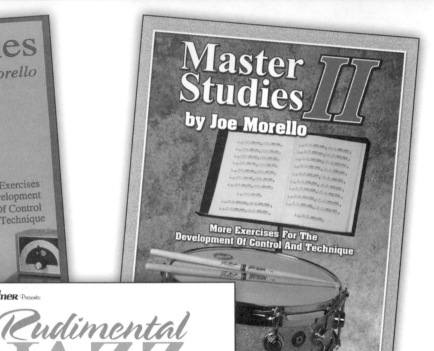

Master Studies

This book focuses on these important aspects: accent studies, buzz-roll exercises, single and double-stroke patterns, control studies, flam patterns, dynamic development, endurance studies, and much more!

Master Studies II

Like Master Studies, this is a workbook of material to use in developing the hands for drumming. Challenging exercises encourage students to learn slow, sensible and accurate practice techniques.

Rudimental Jazz

The precursor to his two most widely used instructional books – Master Studies and Master Studies II – this book covers: techniques such as right and left hand grips, playing position, striking the snare drum & hi-hat and more; beginning exercises; drum beats; teacher's charts; graphic cutouts and more.

Available In Print and Digital Format

BUY FROM YOUR FAVORITE MUSIC RETAILER
CHECK OUT MORE AT MODERNDRUMMER.COM